Morsels of Reflection

Morsels of Reflection

APHORISMS

Rosanna Figna

annotated by Patrizia Bonini

authorHOUSE®

AuthorHouse™
1663 Liberty Drive
Bloomington, IN 47403
www.authorhouse.com
Phone: 1-800-839-8640

First published by AuthorHouse   06/08/2011

ISBN: 978-1-4567-8428-7 (sc)
ISBN: 978-1-4567-8427-0 (ebk)

Printed in the United States of America

MORSELS OF REFLECTIONS WITH VEGETABLES

Note to my readers: *This work is a collection of aphorisms written by me and annotated by a friend.*

If someone is bored, he'll bore you as well: tell him to stop.
*Here it can be noted that the authoress (hereafter known as RF) has a certain respect for the reader. And that she finds it unacceptable to get bored.

It is a really cowardly act to beat a child who's crapping.
*The sentence is strong but denotes the profound culture of RF: the oral, anal, genital phase.

It's true, as Seneca says, that every day we die but that every night we can then resuscitate.
*This is almost mystical. I am reminded of St. John of the Cross and the return to the light.

Is having sex something liberating then? It depends; sometimes it's more liberating to belch.
*RF is from a generation that has given a lot of importance to sex . . . and also knows its limits.

D**kheads can be quite a bit more intoxicating than pure drugs.
*This small gospel reminds us that appearances can be deceptive.

We should never do anything to cheat time; the fact is, it's always time that cheats us.
*We humans—we mortals—are subject to the uncertainties of hours, days, years, and seconds.

Nowadays Snow White probably wouldn't exchange seven dwarves for only one Prince Charming, especially if she knew the dwarves were mine owners.
*The fairytale didn't inform us that the Seven Dwarves were rich.

If there is a gene of intelligence, it's definitely recessive.
*The recessive gene (Mendel's law) is the one that manifests randomly in the genealogical tree. RF is satirical.

There's nothing worse than a hunting dog that gets it into its head to be a guard dog.
*Yes, RF points out a scourge of our times; for example, the Dalmatian, a racing dog that has become a sitting-room dog.

The grass is always greener on the other side of the fence, so dry it well before you smoke it.
*Grass that is very green is full of water and doesn't burn well.

The condom is today's chastity belt.
*Some say that making love with a condom is like having a footbath with socks on.

It's often difficult to know whether we enjoyed ourselves or if others enjoyed themselves because we entertained them.
*RF is one of the most entertaining women to have appeared on the Earth. It's a well-known fact that even Buster Keaton had his sad notes and profound doubts.

No one is a prophet in his own country, especially in Israel, which is the leading world exporter of grapefruit and prophets.
*The origin—the point of this maxim—I firmly believe to be Israel.

Is telepathy an illness of television watching?
*Recent research has confirmed that watching television increases telepathy abilities.

Because of a bit of snow, the city traffic has gone haywire; we need to see what the snow was cut with.
*In the lexicon of the end of the twentieth century and the end of the millennium, *snow* equals white powder, the one that, in certain quarters of Naples, is hurriedly exchanged for cash even before the break of day.

Every man is a forger of his destiny and a cobbler of his own weaknesses.
*This maxim avails itself of profound and vast-reaching figurations: to forge a destiny, and to be able to keep on walking with decent shoes.

The Princess and the Pea is the porn star of fairytales.
*In every sense, the pea under many mattresses is a sign of notable wealth, and porn stars usually earn good salaries.
*[Translator's Note: the Italian word for pea, *pisello*, is also slang for penis.]*

I am a bearer of inner weariness.

Believing is always a good thing; another good thing is believing without obeying or fighting.
*RF is a woman worthy of trust, and that's already a lot, because she knows how to disobey and not fight.

Every time I enter a bank, I dream of robbing it.
*RF comes from a comfortably well-off family. As is well known, the banks have robbed a lot of the rich as well as the poor. This is a thought of vendetta.

The city policeman is someone who, by profession, never minds his own business.
*This profound thought won RF the 'Leopardi-woman prize'—from the worst jadedness, to the viability of pessimism.

Life is a war that should be fought and not suffered.
*The whole meaning of this sentence is taken as read: wars are declared; lives every so often are not.

'Ye were not made to live like unto brutes, But for pursuit of virtue and of knowledge.' Who would credit it, eh!
*The sentence is Dantiesque; it is from *The Divine Comedy* (Inferno: Canto XXVI). *[Dante Alighieri was a major Italian poet in the Middle Ages . . .]*

Now and then, fortune can be self-service; instead, misfortune is always served up at table, even when we haven't ordered it.

Crocodiles cry only on Lacoste™ clothing and accessories.

We should consider our desires the way we consider bullets shot from a gun: don't stand in front of them for no good reason, and remember that they often hit the target.

Have you ever fallen in love with someone who deserves it?
*To understand this question, read Stendhal's *On Love*, De Rougemont's *Love and the Western World*, the letters of Héloïse and Abelard, and R. Barthes' *Fragments discours amoureux* among others.

Slow and steady wins the race? Maybe ... but we thoroughbreds are made for running.
*Profound. Consider also the difference between *excited* and *agitated*, and how many 'racers' are on a stretcher because of it.

Instead of being a hero for a day, I would prefer to be a Messiah for an afternoon.
*It's already happened that in epochal revolutions extreme virtue changes name: from *hero* to *messiah*, for example.

Is it better to be protagonists or spectators? Ideally we would be protagonists, but always with a mirror in front of us so we can watch ourselves.

I know how to resist any temptation, but if it's the temptation that comes looking for me ... well! I certainly can't argue with my destiny!

I own a wardrobe full of dreams; every day I put on a new one.
*For a woman, every dress is a dream, a drop of imagination become fabric, line, colour. Kandinsky and Coco Chanel knew all about such things.

A flower? The perfection of the ephemeral.

Poets shouldn't be industrious about their use of time, but if they have to wait, they too get annoyed!
*Eh, yes, that's right—art, the avant-garde, the relationship between historical and aesthetic time . . . in the meantime we get pissed off.

I'd like to go into lethargy.
*The new race of neurologists has acknowledged that in winter, especially in the northern latitudes, it's better to go into lethargy.

Everyone has his or her *Madeleines*, but no one can make up for lost time.
*The reference is to Proust, an aristocratic author much loved by the Marxists. This is a masterpiece contained in several volumes, which takes a long time to read

I don't know forgiveness; only compassion.

My mind? A precious violin.

Is a dried flower an anorexic flower?

Magic allows us to be reborn to ourselves and remain adolescents.
*By now this is recognized by many psychologists, psychiatrists, psychoanalysts, and other such specialists. Not only is it good to water the adolescence within us, but also the infancy. The authoress expresses a fundamental concept: regression is really progression.

I long for something superior; I don't want to see people prostituting their souls any more.
*We are told this by the poet, the agronomist, the quality control engineer, the writer, Guinness . . . poetry touches mystery.

I belong to that race that is young only once, but immature all its life.
*This sentence is for women as the comment of Che Guevara was for men: 'Without everlosing tenderness.'

Can we grant eternity to a rose? Yes, if we are to believe Paracelsus.
*The rose is the flower *par excellence*, at least in Europe, if for nothing other than the rivers of ink it has caused to gush forth. Recently, I am reminded of G. Stein, L. Irigaray, The Rose Circle of Milan.

I'm a bundle of fascinating defects.

Every flower has its mission to accomplish: it must turn into a seed.
*Many flowers don't accomplish this mission, but fortunately the insects let the pollen fly.

The first biblical scourge is, You will give birth in pain; the second must of course be, You'll awaken violently.
*Many women know this alarming situation. Everything has gone well before sleeping, but there is undoubtedly the morning surprise: the stranger in the bed, or the one who tells you about his life first thing in the morning.

Good manners should never be optional.
*To understand this maxim, read Aries' 'Fathers and Sons,' and the biographies of Jean Rhys, Montessori, Dewey, and others.

Happiness? A full bottle right there, within hand's reach. Pity there's no bottle opener.
*A possible serenity, a skipping joy, a happiness chimerical, or devoid of technique . . .

Have you ever tried to feel perfect?

If I had to make this planet all over again, I'd make it the same, but without mosquitoes.
*Until a short time ago, I would have said 'without flies', but I found myself about to slide into a precipice half asleep and was saved by a fly.

There really is a modern genie's lamp: it's the mobile phone.
*Contemporaneity! Looking around, I see there are many other genie's lamps.

To be happy? To not desire to be anywhere else, in any other way, and with anyone else ... Bingo!

Everything starts with small things; for example, fecundation (Pessoa).

What treaty do we have to sign to have peace for the senses?
*I refer you to an essay by Erasmus of Rotterdam: 'The Complaint of Peace'.

If I had the power to perform miracles, no one would know.

Not all seagulls are like Jonathan Livingston.
*This reference is to the most famous seagull in literature.

Is it the sea that hugs the earth or the earth that goes to kiss it? In any event, it's a fine marriage.
*I am reminded of Rimbaud's: 'La Mer Epousée' and all other mythical, mystical, and mystery cult weddings. When all's said and done, marriage is a sacrament.

No sex appeal will ever be stronger than my dignity.
*See note above.

Carrots are the only vegetables that might feel penis envy.
*This, of course, is a pornographic allusion. It's well known that medium-sized carrots, zucchini, or eggplants are the most common home-spun sex-pleasure gadgets.

To reach a state of grace, is a particular passport necessary?
*In RF's work, the contrast is often present between the dash for freedom and the bureaucratic implication of human hope.

Every now and then I draw the curtains of my mind.

I shall interpose hectolitres of wine between me and my pain.
*Here is a sentence that smacks of feminism. In feminist times, we used to hear, 'I'll interpose mountains of bodies between me and that being ...'

Is petting like jogging?
*They're both a light form of training ...

My life owes sincere thanks to Jethro Tull, Pink Floyd, David Bowie, Peter Gabriel, D. Mode, U2 and ... Nutella.
*And all of us, in the depths of our hearts, agree.

What if Atlantis really existed?

I like sending my mind on holiday.

If you've seen a ghost, don't immediately feel like Hamlet.
*RF's irony is really subtle and post-Oedipus. It might even not be the ghost of Banquo.

Go where sex leads you ...

The essence of old age? It's thinking that the best that could ever have happened to you has already happened ...

On a scale from one to ten, how much do you like yourself? For myself, eleven.
*RF adheres to mathematical numerology, even if knowing how to square things up. Eleven is the number of genius, and two is the number of femininity.

In love, he or she who flees wins, but only if there's someone chasing.

I am free like the wind on the wings of a falcon.
*All of us in the Blue Ladies Frisbee Club adore Frederick II of Sweden and falconers.

Sardinians speak in block letters.
*Not only do they speak with a particular diction, but also their dancing is special. Are their shoes drums?

Summer, time for love! However, we should remember that wounds washed in seawater are the hardest to heal.

After listening to Queen on a cliff top hammered by the wind, I made my will.

Are there more lost opportunities or 'seized' ones?

Coito, ergo sum.
*After Cartesius, after all those who have corrected it with—Mando, ergo ... Bibo, ergo ... Dormio, ergo ... at last!

Sheep already lack strong individualism, but if I were Dolly, I'd have a serious identity crisis.
*Culture is not water! The authoress knows that artificial insemination, test-tube genera, and cloning provoke problems and difficult relationships with the species and with personality determination.

What colour are your divinities?
*RF deserves a prize for merely formulating this question.

If your heart gives in, it's useless beating it.

Sublime sunsets, splendid landscapes, untamed nature . . . however, the most fascinating thing of all are people.
*Yes, that's right, what journeys would there be without the meetings you can have?

And who would you like to be cloned from? From C. Schiffer? From Einstein? Me, from Pablo Neruda.

I'd like to receive some signal from Vega or Alpha Centauri or Pegasus or the Pleiades . . .
*RF has been answered, but still doesn't know how to decipher it.

Trying something often tries our hopes.
*Quality is never an accident, but always a result of intelligent effort.

Are Manicheans a shape of pasta?
The Manicheans have spun many threads, and have given thread to be spun; they have separated good from evil a great deal. Like pasta drainers. [*Manicheans are ancient believers in dualism.*]

We small people often have the strength of Jedi masters.
*For more information, see Adler's theories, the Gospel, and the Star Wars series.

Vulgarity is of no use; however . . . it can help.
*It's a rhetorical figure of great importance. It's similar to what is commonly done when the thought comes that also Edison went to the toilet.

Flowers of evil . . . flower children. By now we're fried flowers.
*This is a pessimistic note of the authoress. In reality, we're not fried flowers; flowers can still be eaten—have you not heard of a violet omelette, or stuffed pumpkin blossoms?

Sometimes I feel like a Siren who has been seduced by Ulysses.

The Corinthians are a people who have received a lot of post. (All those letters of S. Paolo . . .)

I didn't know responsibility towards anyone, until I had a Tamagotchi chick.
*It seems that even the little child we hope is the future empress of Japan should grow up with this sense of responsibility. *[Tamagotchi Electronic Pets are very demanding and require diligent care.]*

Having no time is sometimes not an excuse, but guilt.
*For example, when the authoress loses her rag ...

The story of Cinderella is the 'gospel' of foot fetishists.
*The fetishism of the female foot started in ancient China where even adult women's feet were bound to a length of as little as 12 centimeters (4.72 inches). The history is very long. Another episode occurred in the seventeenth century when ladies who wanted to walk amongst the corpses of the plague victims and still keep their dresses clean and tidy invented the wedge-heeled shoe.

Between a writer and a reader there should be the same relationship that exists between a cook and a diner.
*Then it all depends on the quality of the restaurant ...

Have you got optimist's spectacles? The ones that make everything look rosy?
*Ah, the proverbial rose-colored glasses ...

'If someone offers me some money, in all conscience I don't feel like refusing it.' (Mother Theresa of Calcutta) Wise woman!

We're not all the same, it's true, but someone who has nothing similar doesn't interest me.
*This brings to mind Rousseau's *Discourse on Inequality*, and the much-discussed law: like cures like.

A sport I practise little is sex; however, when it happens, I really apply myself.
*The authoress has discreetly given mankind many passages from this chapter, often under a pseudonym.

I believe in the God Aspirin, Sister Novalgina, Brother Cortisone, and St. Antibiotic—all rapid and efficacious remedies.

The obsessive, the obsessed ... but where's our need for the immense?

The only way to have a lover is to be one.

The disgrace of Cain is unmistakable ... they manage to smite only the Abels—those who don't deserve it.

We grow not only to become adults but also to acquire a certain magnanimity.

I'm in the list of medicines against depression not prescribable under the NHS.

Was it love or an excess of narcissism?
*This is an example of the babble disseminated by the psycho companies. Anyone who realizes this is clever.

Youth wasted. And by what? By boredom probably.
*Here's an anticipation for future studies. Boredom is the worst mortification in a reality full of stimuli. See Illich on 'Boredom in Unemployment.'

In the firmament there is something written for each of us; we should try to read it.
This relates to etymology, astrology, or the sixteen years of today from Chaos to Cosmos in five minutes in front of a drink.

For those who believe, I am a miracle.

Loving is very arduous.
*This thought blends with the ideas of Osho Rajneesh. Because love is arduous, it's impossible to love twenty-four hours a day; it's already a lot if we love for six hours. And then we need to know how to administrate either six hours during the day or six hours during the night.

A good snack is often better than a too eagerly awaited dinner.
*Simplicity. The fruit of exponential reduction by RF. At times a little boiled egg is better than the grand gourmet of Chez Maxime.

Any fiction needs some contact, albeit a small amount, with reality. And any reality needs to be seasoned with imagination.
*I think Milan Kundera would agree.
(MK writer of Czech origin born in 1929)

I've registered my sex with UNESCO: it's a patrimony of mankind.

When we cry, we should have the dignity and good taste to do it alone.
*That is, too many tears sink even the best steamships.

I'd like to link up with the collective unconscious.
*Beyond Jung, perchance who? James Hillman.
Jung (1875-1961), Swiss psychiatrist
Hillman contemporary American psychologist and therapist

I don't see why my body must inexorably age when instead my mind continuously renews itself and gets younger.
*It's a mystery of ministries and of other mysteries.

Between one piece of rotten luck and the next we will become invincible.
*Well-tempered virtue is like a Wilkinson blade.

It's been quite some time since science abandoned the geocentric system, so is it time I abandoned the egocentric one?

Homo sapiens is like *Boletus edulis* (a mushroom); the best part is the head.

Sometimes there are thoughts that are so advanced they have to surpass science and slip into magic.
*With the comforts of science, literature develops its progress beyond.

'There are more things in heaven and earth ... than are dreamt of in your philosophy.' (Shakespeare, *Hamlet*, Act 1, Scene 5).

Why travel? To satisfy our desire for the infinite, given that Ambrose has already seen to the one for something sweet.
*This is a reference to our dear driver, of Milanese origins, and his spot of *chocolathe*.

Women inherit the Earth even without being humble.
*Yes, that's right, it seems the species protects itself ...

The paper of poets is often thirsty for ink, and they themselves for sparkling wine.
*There you are. Artists, poets, and musicians have to keep their spirits up, and Nutella is not enough.

Get your knickers off with joy!

If you really want to hurt yourself, strip off.
*The eye wants to take its part ...

Nude? No-o! Clad in wind, light, and poetry, which is the most beautiful garment there is.
*Wind, light, poetry—a romantic with calculator and computer.

If you have the courage to strip off, do it with style.
*After so much care taken for clothes, which make a comic but also a monk, also stripping is style. See St. Francis.

A soul is truly beautiful when it's naked.
*As above.

The hardest war that's ever been fought is the one between the sexes.
*This is great theme for the end-of-the-school-year exam. Most wars involve tactics and strategies, but the war between the two sexes involves only the difference.

Stupidity is a phenomenon that is unstoppable and inevitable.
*This is the third phase of Leopardian cosmic pessimism.
[Giacomo Taldegardo Francesco di Sales Saverio Pietro Leopardi (1798-1837) was an Italian poet, essayist, philosopher, and philologist.]

I'd like to have a travel agency of the imagination
*Advice of the authoress: A virtual shop? A mirror?

Love is like tuna fish: sometimes it breaks apart with a bread stick.

The dose of foresight each one of us has received is measured when we unpack.
*Is the suitcase of dreams measured when it's unpacked?

Every haystack always contains at least one needle (but this is not demonstrable).
*Seek ... seek the needle in the haystack! You can find it!

Hair lacquer is an aphrodisiac for the hair (it causes the hair to stiffen).
*This is understood as male hair, of course.

Time is our enemy only if we treat it badly

If the devil had made the lids as well as the pans, we would all be hermaphrodites.
*I sense the male is her lid, and she his lid. The sculptress Fiore de Henriquez, who was a hermaphrodite, was perfect.

Cinderella is the progenitor of all domestic helpers.
*The penitential cinder, the blessed pumpkin of the poor, the prince of a state, who is guessed to be of the East, a perennial recipe ...

Puss in Boots would have them today in glossy black varnish with steel high heels, laces, and studs.

Hansel and Gretel would now have a highly renowned beauty farm.
*It would be called General Chocolat or Perfects Candits.

The story of the ugly duckling is the parable of plastic surgery.

Sleeping Beauty is a lady who got the dose of Valium wrong.

Nowadays Pinocchio would be a guest on the *Maurizio Costanzo Show*.
[Maurizio Costanzo (born in 1938) is an Italian television personality and journalist who hosts a famous talk show.]

What if the mountain stayed where it was, and Mahomet stayed where he was?
*Reflection on the Holy Alliance and human beings.

Everything from ancient Sumerian writing can be translated with modern COBOL (Common Business Oriented Language—a programming language) ... but can we then understand?
*COBOL, who was that?

Sometimes I'm like a moth; I can't avoid burning my wings before realizing it was only an artificial light.

Have you ever seen a starry sky, billions of stars, thousands of light years away—a moment in time when everything that exists originated—and infinite space? So why do you get so worked up?

I gave up thinking in September 1985.
*The 'enchantment' concluded with the criticism ...

True love is like gambling; it doesn't worry about the future.
*Ladies and Gentlemen, married couples, reflect upon it.

Who can say and where the present begins?
*From the reflections of St. Augustine to Proust ...

We've already given a lot of answers, but we haven't understood the questions.
*It seems that Gertrude Stein, as she was dying, asked herself precisely what is the question? What is the answer? RF, post-Steinian, places the enigma on a higher plane.

A gurgling fountain says a lot more to me than so many useless words.
*Is it the power of water or the vanity of the discourse?

The only thing that allows a couple to stand each other for life is unfaithfulness.
*The Mysteries of Love multiply, and of these the authoress is a contemporary priestess. It's worth remembering that an understanding and very creative breed of unfaithful lovers was persecuted (I refer to the Cathar Heresy).

Every man, to survive himself, must first traverse the mystery of a woman.
*The ironic accent is placed on 'survive himself', a fundamental question for the male ego.

Life—one's own life—is, at the end of the day, the story one makes of it.
*An extremely up-to date topic, typically Cancerian (cf. H. Hesse). In fact, also the past exists if it can be told.

Making poetry is like making love: you never know whether your joy is being shared.
*There is, it's true, the myth of the simultaneous orgasm in love. It is a rarity. As for poetry, it is said that the gods rejoice.

For people like me, the corner bar is a little Capitol.
*RF is a modern woman, audacious, sporty. As well as throwing herself out of aircraft, winning horse races, and swimming among sharks, she has understood that social life in Italy has its *Via Crucis* stages (stations of the cross). One place, then for everyone, the bar ...

I'd like to cross the river without getting wet.
*The Great Artist would always like to attempt the impossible, to witness the Miracle.

Wanting to catch flies with the buttocks ...
*Another exercise of superhuman ability.

'So the efficient shall be blamed, and he who always obtains a result shall be punished.' (From the gospel of St. Sloth.)
*This is beyond St. Precarious, a dominator of the labor market, who also says, 'No work shall be given to he who likes work.'

Knowledge can be used for only three objectives: to create, to command, and to heal.

Morning rises from below; evening falls from above.
*Like all serious observations made with feet on the ground and eyes open, this should be reflected upon.

I'd like to increase the volume in my life, but I can't find the right knob.
*Many years after Marconi's invention, it's worth reacquiring the language that relates to it: knobs and buttons, turn, press, and pull.

Is putting wings on your feet like putting shoes on dreams?
*This is a marvelous allusion to our lives as shamans, often derided, as was Baudelaire's *The Albatross*, as slovenly …

Certain things happen late to sensitive souls; and never to the insensitive.
*Bear in mind the term *obtuse*, which can refer to both the angle and the man.

Pinocchio told the truth and immediately got his ears boxed.
*We love this puppet made by Geppetto, who was maybe the first to say, 'Let's hope I manage.'

Why are there no more 'white' spaces on the map of the world?
*Yes, this is strange. Still, today we have to wonder whether the ownership of the ground is total or not, and whether notaries still have a sense.

To apologize takes great class.
*Things of great class are much liked. Then they're taught to everyone. It's not the same for the sexual act and apologies.

We should have the wonder of the child and the depth of the elder.
*Can one go with the other? We should ask James Hillman, someone who knows something about *puer* and *senex*. *[Hillman is a contemporary American psychologist who specializes in archetypal psychology.]*

Fuckers, perhaps, we are born; fishermen we can come to be.
*Here, personally, I disagree: we also become fuckers, and we have to apply ourselves more. Fishermen then, it's already something if they're born.

'The difference between stupidity and genius is that genius has its limits.' (Swift)
*Genius is like a limited edition text, by now, moreover, read by very few.

The Kingdom of Heaven belongs to the simple. There you are, I can't go there with my analyst!
*Here's a great statement . . . a draught of pure, angelic air.

He was so presumptuous that, when he got a slap, he turned the other cheek because he believed they had been muddled up.

Americans are possibilists in everything, except fellatio.
*This is an allusion to the event that pricked the democratic conscience of many. A fascinating president, a buxom intern, and a TV show on the trial, which followed the well-known oral act. Did we need planetary certainty?

Is there some beauty in renunciation? It doesn't seem so to me.
*The non-sacrificial hypothesis concerns many currents of thought. After two thousand years, women don't like the sense of guilt any more.

Beautiful women are for men without imagination. (Proust).
*It's well known also that men's imagination is available in limited quantities.

What I look for on the Internet doesn't exist.
*Yes, that's right, Internet . . . what's the use of looking?

We are superior because we have loved.
*It was time the spirit of Magdalene manifested itself before. Before.

Democracy is a dictatorship that changes every four years.
*This saying, in absolute cognition of the facts, could almost be referendary.

Waking up, getting up, is always something difficult . . . think how hard it must have been to resuscitate!
*Oh yes, Lazarus. *Levantate que Dios te quiere vivo.* (Arise because God wants you alive). To obey seems easy.

I don't want to give advice because people know how to make mistakes alone.
*Yes, that's right—everyone knows how to make mistakes; few realize it however.

Utopias? We are realizing them; we just need a bit of time.
*The 'love generation' strikes again, even if a bit late.

Nothing is immobile, certain, definitive. Not even death, as long as there's someone who believes in rebirth.
*RF has made various passages recognizable in the body of her work.

He was so inept an authoritarian he couldn't even get his own shadow to follow him.

I don't know if I'm a genius, but I'm certainly reckless enough.
*The authoress here displays the necessity for the artist's sneer, according to the *dictamen* (opinion) of Carmelo Bene.
[*Carmelo Bene (1937-2002) was an Italian actor, film director and screenwriter.*]

Hide appearances; everyone will be looking for them!
*The artist, the woman, the one with a career, knows this.

If Marat had had a Jacuzzi, he definitely wouldn't have been assassinated.
*Space-time effect: we can think of Charlotte Corday struggling with the bubbles.
[*Marie-Anne Charlotte de Corday d'Armont (1768-1793)was executed for the assassination of Marat.*]

Are you capable of drawing Ulysses' bow? I am, with the power of thought.
*The bow and the archer are Zen.

Perfection is not being without faults: perfection is being forgiven for them.
*Once again RF shows herself to be a wise woman; in fact, 'Well, nobody's perfect!' (This is the famous final line in the film *Some Like It Hot*.).

I'm like an old bottle of Tabasco: once upon a time I was hot and spicy.

It's true that we live one day at a time, but it's also true that we don't live day by day.

We've already seen everything and its opposite, that's why, every time, we can start all over again.

A kiss is always a kiss. It should be received—even the kiss from Judas.
*It's the great fortune of Ferrero's chocolate kiss (Bacio) that it is less demanding than that of Judas.

If you want certainties, buy them.
*In fact, the only certainties we have are those that can be bought.

The reading I prefer is that of the body; it's the most sacred.
*There is a cunnilingus called 'reading the vortex'.

I know how to look on high even without having a God.
*More and more fashionable—from the hole in the ozone onwards—is the equivalence: God/Heaven.

Love is like the sea: beautiful but perilous.
*Love never stops inspiring. It has done so over the centuries, and we hope—or we fear—that it will continue to do so.

Our unconscious has more strategies than General Rommel.
*He is the man nicknamed 'Desert Fox' in World War II.

Freedom is something difficult and burdensome: it's not for everyone.
In fact, there are few who, being free, have lived beyond fifty.
'They know who for her sake have life refused.' (Dante Alighieri—*The Divine Comedy,* Purgatory: Canto I)

I talk a lot because I have to chase after my thoughts.
*The Light and the Word.

I'd like to fill my solitude the way one fills a gastronomically perfect *panettone*—with every sort of titbit.

If you're near sunset, you like dawns.

Advice always leaves a mark, even if we decide not to follow it.

I know how to thank even those who don't leave me unscathed.
*Do you want to thank your lovers? That's some high class.

MORSELS OF REFLECTION
WITH RHUM CASSANDRA

I have the shoes to walk through myriad worlds.
*More than shoes, it seems that today we should talk of 'strings' as physics would have it . . . 'string theory.'

We have four million years of evolution in these senses of ours; we have to make them work well!
*The wisdom of the body is such that it knows more than we do, by at least four million years.

A fortress that is all wall doesn't interest me.
*This is an allusion to the fascination of the oriental warrior to our own homespun castle with its drawbridge.

All through the long night of Saint Lawrence I see the stars fall. I'll teach you to see them rise again.

At times poetry or art reaches perfection—like the Phoenix when it burns. At times sex reaches perfection too.

I am a guardian of the Promised Time.
*RF is *semper fidelis* with regard to hope—always faithful. *Semper fidelis* is also the motto of the U.S. Marines.

What role has humanity—the human race—had in the expansion of the Universe?
*In the expansion I wouldn't know; in the comprehension, a little more.

If your horizons are vast, your thoughts will be too.
*People who travel over many horizons don't always have vast thoughts . . . look at mass tourism.

'A bird and a feather in the bush is worth more than ten birds in the hand.' (Khalil Gibran). We need to see what bird we're talking about!
*And what hands! *[Gibran (1883-1931) was a Lebanese American writer and artist.]*

'To be irreplaceable, you have to be different.' (Coco Chanel). A great woman!
*Coco's life is something to dream of: she gave us little changes that revolutionized life, like trousers instead of a skirt. *[Chanel (1883-1971) was a very cool French fashion designer.]*

Astrology: the epoch when the celestial bodies have something to communicate to us isn't over yet, especially for those who know how to live in harmony with the Whole. (*Astra inclinant, non necessitant*—The stars incline; they do not determine.)
*That is to say, the stars may influence us, but they aren't ineluctable!

'Sunday flattens out the creases of the whole week.' (Joseph Addison) Fortunately this is also true for Saturday.
*At the current level of creases, Friday too cuts a fine figure!
[Addison (1672-1719) was an English writer and politician.]

Beauty is in the eye of the beholder. Is that why the handsome are ogled longer?

The people should be protected from the government.
*A first-rate democracy is one in which the citizen can be involved in politics for five minutes and then just forget all about it.

'It's often in hours of relaxation well spent that man finds the entrance to the world.' (Henry Adams). Women find similar entrance!
*Well, if we think of Courbet's *L'Origine du Monde* (*The Origin of the World*), women have the entrance incorporated.

Esse est percepi—To be is to be perceived.

What game do you fancy playing? I'm up for any challenge as long as I can wear a girdle and high heels ... The courage to be, the courage in appearing ...

One being only can't satisfy our need for love.
*Are more needed? Husbands and fiancés start taking note.

The ego is all right, but dressed in light clothes.

The fruits of passion ... many have never tried it!
*A fruit that's difficult to pick and doesn't last.

I've done my catechism with Don Lurio.
*Don Lurio is the Don of dancers, as well as a choreographer and Italian TV presenter. His catechism is the pirouette with 'Voilà!' finale and outstretched hand.

My sense of justice often surpasses the rules, the laws, and also the fines.

Gluttony, Pride, Anger, Sloth, Lust, Envy, Greed. I don't get it; apart from Greed and Envy, they're all virtues.
*I'd like to add Pride to the two mentioned above: an ego with a platinum coat

The great works of static engineering of this epoch have been the Eiffel Tower, the Empire State Building, the skyscrapers of Kuala Lumpur . . . and the chignon of Moira Orfei.
*Moira is a name that is already a complete programme (the Moires, goddesses of Fate). Can her chignon have inspired mom Simpson? *[Moira Orfei is a popular circus performer, actress and TV personality with an atypical hairstyle.]*

He who lives in hope, dies singing.
*The story of Pandora's box explains that elusive hope lies at the bottom. Better off singing!

What a relief not to do the things people expect of you.

Spinning around your Self like a top is not only useless, but sometimes harmful too.
*Dancing round the whole room, like the Sufi and F. Battiato want us to do is okay as long as there's no furniture. *[Franco Battiato is an Italian singer-songwriter.]*

How come there are always pre-packaged questions for which you have to press button one, two, or three? And what if the one you want to ask isn't in the plan?

Is it possible to remain indifferent in front of a blossoming cherry tree?
The fascinating always makes an impression . . .
*RF recalls yamatology, Shinto: what colour are cherry flowers?

If only I could found cities, I would rebuild Sodom and Gomorra.
*Instead I'd re-build Alexandria.

The soul of jokes is eternally young.
*RF recalls figures known in myth: the Rogue, the Rogue Goddess.

Politics helps those involved in it a great deal.
*It's been noticed that politics is an effective resource against certain unemployment.

The source of youth ... does it come in a bottle?
*I think RF proposes herself as consumer of the mythical product.

Does the bill include merriment value?
*This added value is one of the most appreciated, but least refunded.

There are no more absolute Truths: even the Gospels were written by four evangelists ... who would have formed a rock band in this day and age.

UFOs. We'd like them to identify themselves.

When you feel like having a crap, nothing else matters.

May every morning bring the unusual!

If you listen carefully to the backwash of the sea, every wave has its own sound.

He who doesn't know how to apologise pays twice.

I'm training to become a Mahatma.
*Everyone's training in something—in tennis, at the gym . . . RF trains in subaqueous immersions, equitation, poetry and literature, humour and transcendence, juggling, friendship, agronomy and mass alimentation, and more. Last but not least, she trains in the introduction of sex in the spirit of narration, because training to be a 'great breath' or Mahatma means above all to prepare yourself in several spheres.

Christmas should follow us all year round: the desire to give presents, the surprise at receiving them, the sense of wonder in front of trees that nature decorates on its own, the sensation of the festivity and the longing to celebrate it. Then, above all, that desire to sit down in front of a nice plateful of *zampone* (traditional stuffed pig's trotter—thanks!) and mashed potatoes even in the summer . . . Happy Christmas!
*Yet we used to say, "Survive Christmas!"

A boss, in addition to magnanimity, must also possess a good dose of humility.

He who surrenders has finished losing.
*This thought of RF is equal to thoughts of Chuang Tzu—ancient Chinese philosopher: running, random victory . . . losing remains, and this is the respect for struggle.

Social cohabitation is never painless.
*This dilemma involves Aristotelians and others; I mean to say, is man a social animal or not? And if he is, how come cohabiting politically ends up being so burdensome?

We cry alone, but when we laugh, it's better to do so in company: a laugh should always be shared.
*A laugh is willingly shared, at times even with the foolish.

Are there any hydrofoils we can take to the Island of Utopia?

In love and war, sometimes bridges have to be breached: the important thing is not to produce dead or wounded.

Captain Nemo could have made masses of fish soup with all that octopus!

Sexual desire is perpetual and oscillating—like the movement of the pendulum.

Fireworks produce a light that follows the force of gravity.
*Sure enough!

If people were to ask themselves more questions—to ask themselves "why"—there would be much more serenity. It's on the surface that the waters are often agitated; in the depths there is calm and comprehension.

I went into a motorway café for a cappuccino, and I came out with a biography of Julius Caesar. Is it the power of history, the aura of the personage, or am I just getting sillier?

How beautiful summer is! With the heat, all the windows are open. Do you hear that fine concert of belches echoing round the block of flats!

It's gratifying and important to ask ourselves questions that surpass the barrier of the centuries; for example, "Would Napoleon have been a handsome man?"
*Or why is it that all—or almost all—ancient statues have lost their noses? And why is Cleopatra's so often talked about?

In Nature, there is the perfection of the infinitely small; however, the same cannot be applied to the male attributes.

Sex has reasons that Reason doesn't know at all.
*Here's a paraphrase of Pascal: In fact, sex has consequences that are not always predictable or controllable. Moreover this also happens to dolphins, cats, dogs, horses . . . and spiders? I mean to say, it's a risk of nature.

Is the happiness of a genius the same as the happiness of the common man?
*In this question is a shadow of Romanticism. Nowadays I wouldn't bet on the happiness of the common man. The last well-known genius, A. Einstein, must have felt fairly happy when he stuck his tongue out at the photographers!

He who is seeking the other half of the apple must take care it hasn't gone rotten.

Do you already know what questions to ask the extraterrestrials?
*There are those who already see them among the people, and we're not dealing with 'nutters'. There is a website for those who have been contacted, and there are many specialists in crop circles. We should prepare ourselves for a shocking appearance—as in the film *Men in Black*. We're in rather a bad way—what could we really sell the aliens?

Venture capitalist . . . what if we were still to ask for a pound of flesh in exchange as in Shakespeare's *Merchant of Venice*?
*Also the venture capitalist is identified by, and complicated by the fact that money is almost intangible—numbers that are to

be found in who-knows-which bank. Just to say that we don't know the relationship between the figure and the steak.

To all those seeking the Holy Grail . . . you can find it in a jar of Nutella!
*RF has passed through the culture of TV commercials and public service advertising. Today's twelve-year-olds find the commercial breaks more interesting than the programmes themselves. The power of Nutella!

Sometimes even Master Yoda doesn't know what to do. There are those who were born on the dark side of the Force!
*A lot of things say that the end of time is near: The earth will turn on itself once, but from north to south. There will be a deformation of the dark and light side. Anyone left will have understood how to spend their days. On the light side, with clear waters and skies, we might find ourselves eating good bread and drinking good wine, loving, and singing along with the survivors. Then Master Yoda won't have any doubts: "If you well have done, in these days here will you be." [*Yoda is a Jedi Master in the Star Wars film series.*]

In regression there is often much progress.
*The child within us . . . *para siempre* (for always!)!

There is always a *kairos*—a propitious moment in which to realize the imagined.

At times I have the courage of one who believes himself immortal.

Even the Jedi knights are often ill-prepared for the difficult task of living well.
[Yet another reference to the Star Wars film series.]

Perhaps one day the White Rabbit will stop running and looking at his watch and repeat, "I'm in a hurry, I'm in a hurry." Then he will sit himself down quietly to drink a beer.

I like digesting.
*Digesting is a bodily pleasure; doing it with the typical emissions of sounds from a block of flats is called belching, a little like the mouth of the volcano releasing its gas.

A ghost is always the relic of a remorse?

I've enrolled in the Reincarnation Society; you never know . . .

Reasoning with the hormones instead of the neurons can be fun.
*Hormone and Neuron are the two great protagonists of our era: Hormone is the son of Joy; Neuron is the son of Conscience. Even if they come from two different mothers, they are mono-ovular twins who are quite different . . . a mystery of pataphysical mythology.

In hunting, the pleasure of giving death exorcises the fear of receiving it.

The face is the mirror of the soul, but with all this plastic surgery, it's become a bit disoriented!
*We recall the popular broadcast on 'new monsters'—gorgeous women, all queens of Snow White, who confused their own images with the surgeon's mirror.

Never trust anyone too much. Even God, when he was much believed in, created some disasters!

Every conflict is always preceded by an encounter, generally of equal intensity.

Everyone is a messiah to himself.
*We are all free to consecrate ourselves to our own beings.

At times I'm aware of the deaths I have passed through in previous lives.

Girls, always wash your feet well before going out; you never know whether you're going to meet Prince Charming who wants you to try on a shoe!
*Yes, girls, let's update the terrible fairytale once more: the first tiny shoe was made for the wife of a Chinese prince, who liked feet to be twisted and soft. The second tiny shoe

was made of glass, and you can imagine the effect of that on tender feet! With the advent of high fashion, Cinderella could choose shoes of cloth hardened with glue. After Jacqueline Onassis, she could choose plimsolls to wear while jumping onto yachts. Now a flip-flop could be enough. But the skin of the foot needs careful pumice stoning and perfuming, perhaps with balsam. In looking after your feet then, try not to neglect the hairs, so-called superfluous ...

May your thoughts unfurl like parables from the Gospels ... unfurl like sails in the wind.

The non-reply—silence—is a perennial fuck off.

In the smile of the Mona Lisa lies an awareness of the immortality of art.
*The enigmatic smile of the Gioconda was Leonardo's favourite work, which he always carried with him. In fact, all painters carried out their small vendettas against their descendents, given that they were forced to frequent the company of people who, for the most part, understood nothing about their work. Hitting a nice mystery on the head really is a great stroke of genius!

Always bring some seeds or a seedling from the places you enjoyed; happiness can sprout everywhere.

If you meet Eros on your road, try to follow him. Coming across a god isn't easy.

Why hide if no one is looking for you?

In beauty—in any beauty—there is always a promise of happiness.

Art is not for the masses . . . and maybe not even these morsels . . .

End

Author Biography

Rosanna Figna lives and works in Parma, Italy, in the middle of the Italian Food Valley. Like Hemingway, she was born on 21 July. She may not write as well as he did, but she drinks a lot less. After Liceo (Italian secondary school) specialising in classical studies, she graduated in agrarian science from the University of Bologna.

Rosanna's books have been published by Italian publishing houses and her short stories have appeared in various authors' collections and reviews (for example, *Playboy*, Italian edition, March 2011). She has won quite a number of literary contests.

She writes because writing is a good substitute for sex and because she's done so since she was a child.

For a living, Rosanna deals with quality control and research and development for a milling company. She loves the sea, and in summer she goes sailing every weekend in her little boat. She also goes scuba diving whenever possible.